AF442171

WHAT ARE AMPHIBIANS?

Animal Book Age 8 Children's Animal Books

Speedy Publishing LLC

40 E. Main St. #1156

Newark, DE 19711

www.speedypublishing.com

Copyright 2017

All Rights reserved. No part of this book may be reproduced or used in any way or form or by any means whether electronic or mechanical, this means that you cannot record or photocopy any material ideas or tips that are provided in this book.

In this book, we're going to talk about Amphibians. So, let's get right to it!

WHAT ARE AMPHIBIANS?

When scientists study animals, they separate them into classes by their characteristics. Amphibians are one of these classes. Reptiles and birds are other classes of animals. You belong in one of the classes of animals too. You are a mammal.

Amphibians hatch from eggs like birds and reptiles do. When they first hatch, they swim in water and have fins like fish. As they grow, they go through a process of change called metamorphosis. During metamorphosis, they form legs and then they can walk on land too.

AMPHIBIANS ARE COLD-BLOODED ANIMALS

Just like snakes, which are reptiles, and goldfish, which are fish, amphibians are cold-blooded. This just means that their bodies don't have the ability to heat up or cool down their internal temperature.

Tadpole

Frog

If a frog feels too hot, it might have to jump in the water to cool down. On the other hand, if it feels too cold, it might have to find a sunny spot to soak up some heat.

THE LIFE CYCLE OF AN AMPHIBIAN

Frogs, toads, salamanders, and newts are all types of amphibians and they each go through a process of metamorphosis. To study an example of how this process of change happens, we're going to look at a frog's life cycle.

Red Spotted Newt

Frogs are very successful at surviving. There are over 4,000 species of frogs, and fossils prove that they've been on Earth for over 200 million years. They're found in marshy swamps all over the world. Frogs must have water to lay their eggs.

Once they hatch from the eggs, for a while they have tails, and swim in the water just like fish do. Let's pretend you have an aquarium and you can watch a frog grow from when it hatches out of its egg to when it becomes an adult frog.

Frog with tadpoles

Frog and Frogspawn

HOW MANY EGGS DO FROGS LAY?

Depending on its species, a female frog will lay hundreds or thousands of eggs.

During the process of mating, the male frog will fertilize the eggs. The eggs are held by an egg sac. It has a jelly-like substance that provides food for the frog embryos. If the egg sacs were deposited in a swamp in the wild, just a few frog eggs would live to be adults. That's because lots of fish and other sea creatures like to eat frog eggs. But, in an aquarium, lots of the frogs will hatch. The egg stage is the first stage of a frog's life.

Tadpoles

WHAT IS A TADPOLE?

When the frog comes out of the egg, it doesn't look anything like an adult frog yet. At this stage, it's a tadpole, which comes from the Middle English words for "toad" and "head." That's exactly how they look, like big heads with tiny tails.

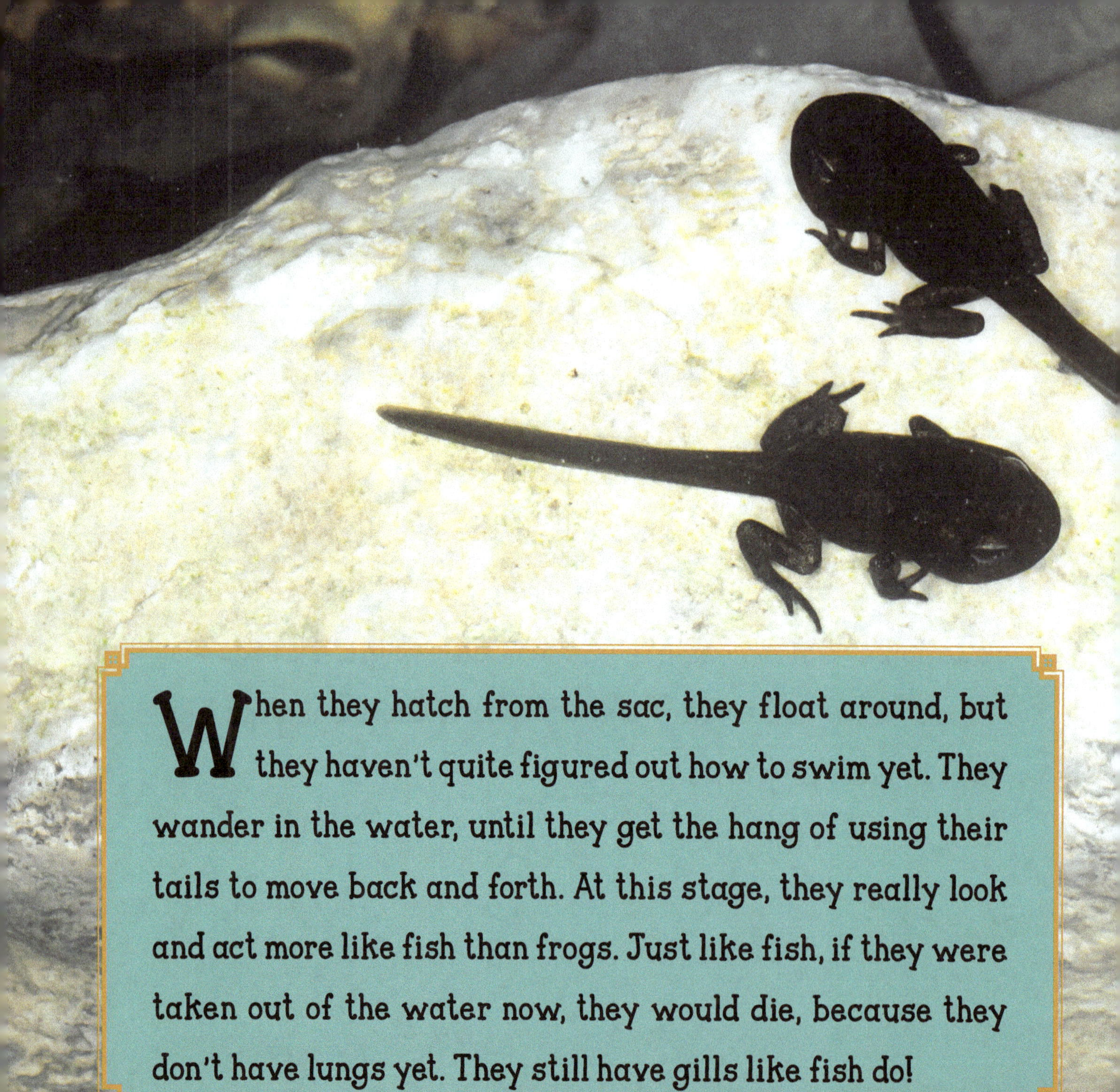

When they hatch from the sac, they float around, but they haven't quite figured out how to swim yet. They wander in the water, until they get the hang of using their tails to move back and forth. At this stage, they really look and act more like fish than frogs. Just like fish, if they were taken out of the water now, they would die, because they don't have lungs yet. They still have gills like fish do!

Tadpoles

If you were feeding them, you'd have to give them plenty of algae to eat, because they are herbivores. That just means they eat plants. They have huge appetites because they have to get ready to change into frogs! This tadpole stage is the second stage of a frog's life.

WHICH LEGS DO TADPOLES GROW FIRST?

Tadpoles grow their hind or back legs first and this is when the big changes start. It's a good thing they ate a lot of food to get ready, because they can't eat anything while their bodies are going through this big change. First, their gills change into lungs. During this part of the process, they have the ability to absorb oxygen right through their skin. Their whole digestive system changes too. Before they could only eat plants, but now their systems change so they can eat insects when they become adult frogs.

Tadpole

The mouths get larger and their tongues get longer. Their jawbones start to grow. Soon, their front legs start to grow. The very final part of this stage is when their tails start to become part of their bodies. Soon they won't have tails at all anymore!

WHEN DOES A TADPOLE BECOME A FROGLET?

Once this part of the metamorphosis is over, the tadpole is now a froglet. The froglet is smaller than an adult frog would be. It also has a stubby tail on its body although most of its tail is gone by now. It still isn't ready to come out of the water yet. It's really hungry after not eating for so long, so it starts to eat plants and insects too.

Froglet

HOW LONG DOES IT TAKE FOR A TADPOLE TO CHANGE INTO A FROG?

Depending on the frog species, it can take just a few weeks to several months or several years for tadpoles to turn into frogs. Eventually, their tails completely disappear and then they are ready to hunt for food on land. Their lungs can breathe air now and they have powerful back legs to jump away from danger. They also blend well into the color of their surroundings so that they can stay safe from other animals that want to eat them.

THE STAGES OF CHANGES

In summary, a frog's life goes through these stages.

Stage 1: The egg is getting
nourishment from the egg sac.

Stage 2: The tadpole hatches and has a head, a long tail, and gills.

Stage 3: The tadpole grows
two back legs.

Stage 4: The tadpole grows two front
legs and its gills change into lungs.

Stage 5: The tadpole is now a froglet with a shorter tail.

Stage 6: The frog is now a full-grown adult and can live on land as well as swim in the water. It eats plants and insects and breathes air.

IDENTIFYING TYPES OF AMPHIBIANS

Frogs and Toads

Frogs and toads, which are a specific type of frog, are both groups of amphibians. Usually they have short bodies with fingers and toes that are webbed. Their eyes bulge and when they are full-grown adults they don't have tails. The American bullfrog is an example of a frog.

Bullfrog

Spotted Salamander

Salamanders

The bodies of salamanders look something like lizards, but they are amphibians not reptiles like lizards are. Their bodies are skinny and they have short legs. They have tails even in their adult stage. If they lose a leg or arm they can regrow it. Newts are a subcategory of salamanders.

Caecilians

Caecilians don't have legs. They don't have arms either. They look similar to worms or snakes but they are amphibians. Some species grow to 4 feet in length! Their skulls are strong and they have noses that are pointed so they can dig through muddy ground.

Caecilian

WHERE DO AMPHIBIANS LIVE?

Amphibians can live anywhere where there are bodies of water available. They live near streams, bogs, and swamps. You can also find them in ponds, lakes, and in rainforests.

WHAT DO THEY EAT?

The larvae of many amphibian species only eat plants, but as adults many amphibians eat both plants and animals. They have a varied diet that includes spiders, worms, and beetles. Some frog species capture their prey with long, sticky tongues.

Giant Salamander

THE BIGGEST AND THE SMALLEST

The biggest amphibian on Earth is the Chinese Giant Salamander, which grows as large as 6 feet in length and can weigh more than 135 pounds! The biggest frog is called the Goliath Frog after the giant Goliath in the Bible. Its body length can be more than 15 inches and it can weigh as much as 8 pounds.

The tiniest amphibian on Earth is a frog that has the scientific name paedophryne amanuensis. It was just discovered in 2012 in New Guinea and it easily fits on a dime at about 0.27 inches long.

FASCINATING FACTS ABOUT AMPHIBIANS

- All species of amphibians have gills for breathing. Some only have them at the larvae stage and others have them for their entire lifespan.

- Frogs can't eat anything larger than their mouths or stomachs because they don't chew their food. They swallow it whole.

- It's completely untrue that you can get warts if you touch a toad.

- Because the skin on amphibians absorbs both air as well as water, pollution is very deadly to them. The world's populations of amphibians are decreasing because of this.

- All amphibians are vertebrates because they have backbones. Even the tiny paedophryne amanuensis!

- Most amphibians have very thin skin. Their skin stays moist in damp environments and helps them breathe.

Awesome! Now you know more about Amphibians. You can find more Animal books from Baby Professor by searching the website of your favorite book retailer.

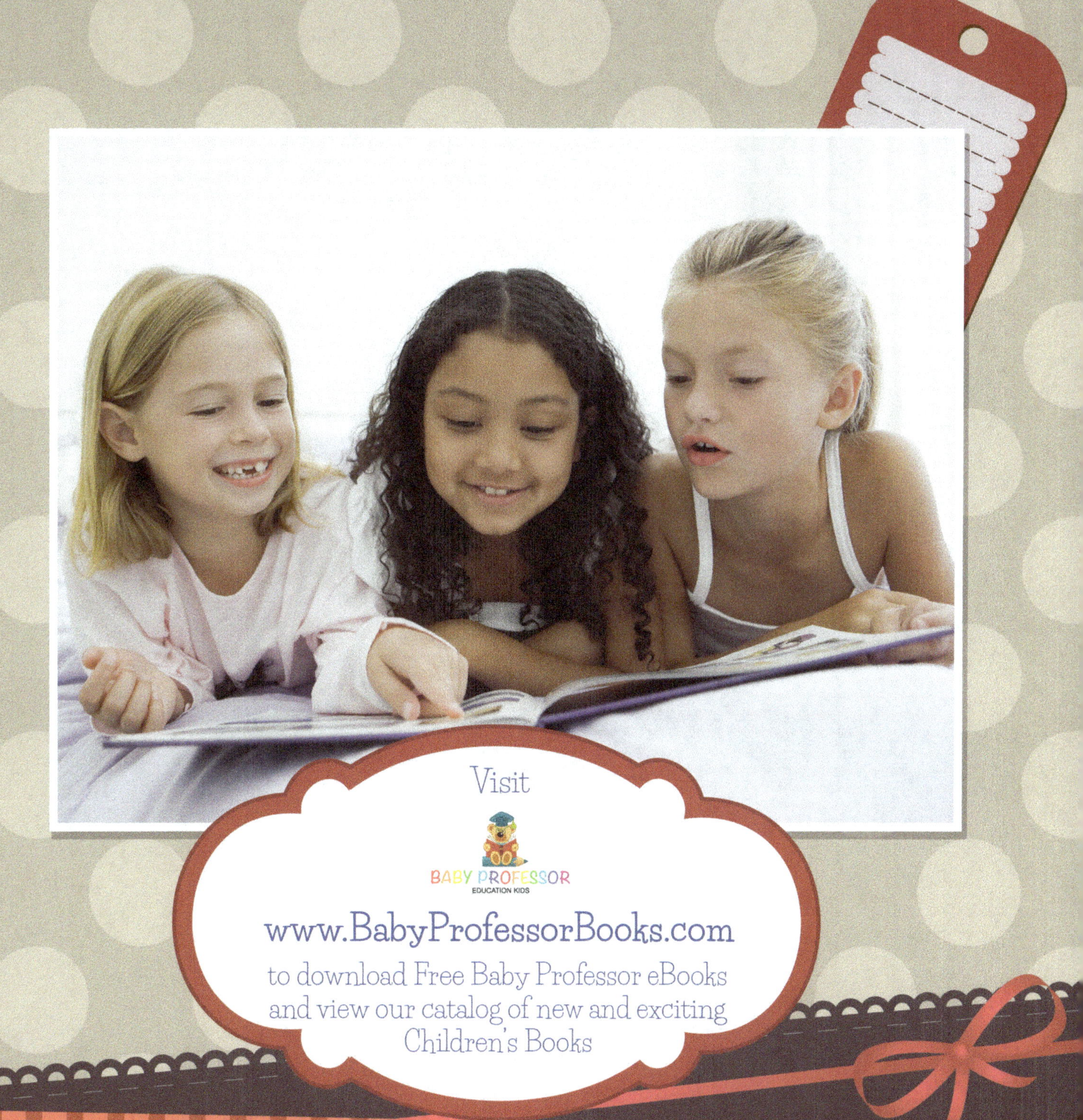

Visit
BABY PROFESSOR
EDUCATION KIDS
www.BabyProfessorBooks.com
to download Free Baby Professor eBooks
and view our catalog of new and exciting
Children's Books

www.ingramcontent.com/pod-product-compliance
Lightning Source LLC
Chambersburg PA
CBHW081148180726
48003CB00026B/2934